POCKET IMAGES

Rumney and the Wentlooge Level

This book is dedicated to the memory of my father who lived all his life in Rumney.

Clifford Henry North
1924-1994

Rumney and the Wentlooge Level

Geoffrey A. North

NONSUCH

Cover picture: A St Mellons village outing in the early 1920s.

First published 1997
This new pocket edition 2006
Images unchanged from first edition

Nonsuch Publishing Limited
The Mill, Brimscombe Port,
Stroud, Gloucestershire, GL5 2QG
www.nonsuch-publishing.com

Nonsuch Publishing is an imprint of Tempus Publishing Group

© Geoffrey A. North, 1997

The right of Geoffrey A. North to be identified as the Author
of this work has been asserted in accordance with the
Copyrights, Designs and Patents Act 1988.

British Library Cataloguing in Publication Data.
A catalogue record for this book is available from the British Library.

ISBN 1-84588-312-8

Typesetting and origination by Nonsuch Publishing Limited
Printed in Great Britain by Oaklands Book Services Limited

Contents

Foreword   6

Introduction   7

1.   Rumney – the Village   9

2.   Rumney at School   33

3.   Rumney at Work   43

4.   Rumney at Prayer   53

5.   Rumney in Uniform   59

6.   Rumney at Play   69

7.   Leaving Rumney and onto the Level   85

8.   Marshfield and Castleton   95

9.   St Mellons   105

10.   Llanrumney   119

11.   Returning to Rumney   123

Foreword

It was with pleasure that I accepted the invitation to write the foreword to this pictorial history of Rumney and the Wentlooge Level. It offers me the perfect opportunity to congratulate Geoffrey North on his work in collating all the old photographs and historical notes to be found in this interesting book.

Photographs can, of course, only portray comparatively recent times, mainly the present century, but the 'known' history of the area goes back at least as far as the Norman period and, to a lesser extent, the Romans.

Rumney and District Local History Society is delighted to be associated with this book and to have made some contribution to what will surely be a successful publication.

Sam Parker
Honorary Secretary
Rumney & District History Society

Introduction

Compiling this book on Rumney and the Wentlooge Level for the Archive Photograph Series has given me much pleasure and an opportunity to share with the reader the many postcards and family photographs I have collected over the years of the area where I was born and brought up.

As a child I was fascinated by the rich history of the area and, despite having moved away because of work, my interest in Rumney and the Wentlooge Level has not diminished. I frequently visit my family who still live in Rumney and many of the photographs included in this volume bring back special memories to me of my childhood. Because of the restriction on space available, selecting the images has been especially difficult and many photographs which I would have liked to include have had to be omitted from this volume. Where possible I have used the older photographs to illustrate how the area has developed since the turn of the century. I am particularly indebted to the many friends, too numerous to mention individually, who have generously helped me by loaning precious photographs or who have taken the time to answer my many questions. Also, a special thank you to the Rumney History Society for their support and encouragement.

My interest in Rumney really starts with its history from the twelfth century but it should be mentioned that some evidence exists of Roman occupation in the area. In the twelfth century the Norman Marcher lords built fortified manor houses to protect themselves from the Welsh and one such house, or castle, was built at Rumney where a settlement developed. The castle was known to have been on the site of Ty Mawr farm but all that now remains of the castle and farm are two roads - Ty Mawr Road and Ty Mawr Avenue - which run through what was once farmland.

In the early twelfth century Rompney (Rumney) also boasted two mills which are frequently mentioned in manorial records. Substantial sums of money were spent on their upkeep and on several occasions the mills were the target of attacks by the Welsh. The last recorded incident was in 1316 when several of the inhabitants were killed.

The oldest buildings remaining in Rumney are St Augustine's church, Beili Bach Cottages and Rumney Pottery. The site and layout of St Augustine's remains essentially unaltered since the first church was built at the beginning of the twelfth century. Although the tower, which was added in the fifteenth century, is similar to many throughout Glamorgan, I believe that it adds to the simple charm of the church. Beili Bach Cottages, where some of my relatives lived at the turn of the century, have now been modernised and are no longer in the state of decay that I remember as a child. The pottery stands at the bottom of Rumney Hill near the bridge and, although boats no longer navigate the river to the quay, it is easy to imagine the importance of the site throughout the history of Rumney.

Because of the nature of this publication it is not possible to cover the history of the area much before the turn of this century but the area is steeped in a wealth of history that should not be ignored and I hope that readers of this volume are encouraged to make the effort to find out more about the area.

This book starts its journey to the west at Rumney Bridge and explores the village where I enjoyed my childhood and continues along 'the lower road' over the level via Peterstone to Marshfield and Castleton before returning along 'top road' to Rumney via St Mellons and Llanrumney.

The most important aspect of any village, however, is its people and I have been especially pleased to be able to include so many photographs of Rumney people of all ages over a period of almost one hundred years.

I very much hope that you will have as much enjoyment in reading this book as I have had in compiling it.

Geoffrey A. North
May 1997

One

Rumney – The Village

Looking towards Rumney Hill from the west, c. 1900, prior to the development of the 'common'.
William Cubitt's house – Castlefield – can be seen at the foot of the hill to the left
of the photograph.

Ernie Giles is seen here *c.* 1955 on the Cardiff side of the River Rhymney digging clay for use at Rumney Pottery. Rumney Bridge can be seen at the top left of picture.

Rumney Bridge, *c.* 1910. William Cubitt's house can be seen to the rear of the bridge. To the right is the old toll-house, the site of which is now included in the grounds of Rumney Pottery. Much evidence exists to suggest that the River Rhymney was crossed at this point as early as Roman times. Certainly, the bridge has always played an important part in the history of Rumney. At the time of the Chartist Riots in Newport in 1839, a detachment of dragoons was placed at the bridge in order to defend Cardiff.

The pottery has been home to the Giles family for more than three hundred years. In 1884, when a photographer was still a novelty, many residents of Rumney posed for this picture; even the village policeman can be seen here in what is thought to be the earliest photograph taken of the pottery.

Members of the Giles family are pictured here turning pots at Rumney Pottery in the 1950s.

Rumney pottery in the early 1920s. Although many of the outbuildings seen here have now been demolished, the character of the pottery has changed little over the years.

Pearl, Vera and Renie Giles holding pitchers and water carriers for sale at the pottery in the 1950s.

Rumney Hill, c. 1935, looking towards the 'common' and beyond towards Cardiff. The twin towers of Roath power station can be seen in the background. It is thought that the power station was the intended target of the bombs dropped on Rumney during the Second World War. Thankfully there were no casualties in the raids although some damage to property resulted.

Newport Road, looking east towards the Carpenters Arms, c. 1964. Stan Phillips' butcher's shop, together with Chapman's post office and stores can be seen on the right. Although the shops have changed hands little else appears to have altered in more than thirty years.

Further east along Newport Road, *c*. 1916. The Rumney Dairy & Café can be seen on the right. The trees on the left have long since disappeared but the view is still easily recognisable.

The Carpenters Arms advertising Ritchies draught ale, *c*. 1940. This public house remains a popular inn with the residents of Rumney today.

Newport Road at its junction with Wentlooge Road, looking west towards the Carpenters Arms, c. 1932. A chemist's shop occupied the corner position for many years. The entrance to Rumney Court can be seen to the right of the picture.

Rumney Court, pictured here c. 1920, was once the home of Richard England, a successful importer and distributor of potatoes. The Court is now home to the British Legion Club.

Although the actual occasion is not known, seen in this photograph dating from c. 1932 are Squire Williams, Thomas Batten, Miss Simons of Witla Court, W.E. ('Bagsy') Jones of Ty Mawr farm and Leighton Seager of Hillcrest. The Griffin family of Rumney Court is also represented.

At the turn of the century, Rumney post office was to be found at the top of Wentlooge Road, close to the site of the County Cinema.

Church farm, which stood at the junction of Tyr y Sarn Road and Church Road, pictured here *c.* 1895. The farmhouse was demolished in 1937.

The Batten family farmed Church farm for many years. In this photograph Gwen Rees (*née* Batten) can be seen about to climb onto the cart, *c.* 1920.

Looking towards St Augustine's parish church from the site of Church farm c. 1966. A bungalow now occupies the original site of the farmhouse.

These young children playing in Ty Fry Road in 1906 are believed to be members of the Fantham family.

Ty Fry Cottages, then home of the Fantham family, *c.* 1910.

Mrs Fantham in Ty Fry Road in 1915 with her family: Doris, Gladys, Iris, Chrissie, Mona, Rommie, Charlie and Harry.

Ty Mawr Road shortly after the building of Rumney Baptist church and before the road had been completed. The building of the new church started on 9 April 1929 when the first sod was cut by James Summers.

Brachdy Road, c. 1918. Arthur Scrivens is seen lying in the road next to Charles Turner. The group of children on the right include Edna Turner and Joan Wilson. The two young ladies walking down the road are Gladys Roberts and Edith Gerrish.

Beili Bach Cottages with the tower of St Augustine's church in the background, *c.* 1969.

Beili Bach Cottages, *c.* 1938.

Left: Mrs Mary Andrews (*née* Bower – my great-great-grandmother). The Bowers originated from a long-established Gloucestershire family. Mary is pictured here at Beili Bach where she lived at the turn of the century.

Below: Orchard Terrace, which now forms part of Wentlooge Road, *c.* 1920. The Rompney Castle can be seen to the centre of the picture.

Slightly further down Wentlooge Road at its junction with Cae Glas Avenue and Brachdy Road, c. 1900. The Rompney Castle is in the background.

The lane pictured here in 1966 passes over what was once Church farm and leads from Wentlooge Road to Church Road at its junction with Tyr y Sarn Road. It was a favourite short cut home from school in my childhood.

Although the location of this photograph taken around the turn of the century is unknown, many of today's Rumney families are represented. Included in the group are Lizzie Vincent, Tom Gerrish, Stanley Truscott, Billy Morgan, Jack Vincent, Joe Marsh, Tommy Andrews, Annie Gear, George North, Jane North (née Andrews) and John North. The young child, second from the right in the front row, is Milly Whatley.

A Standard motor car outside the Memorial Hall, Wentlooge Road, *c.* 1960. The hall was opened in 1924 by the Marchioness of Bute as a memorial to the men of Rumney who fell in the First World War. It cost £2,359 to build and has been home to a baby clinic, crèche, dance and drama club, slimming club as well as numerous other groups including the army cadets. The village library was housed at the rear of the hall from 1938 to 1973.

My mother Jean North (*née* James) pushing me along Wentlooge Road in a Silver Cross pram, *c.* 1950. In the background can be seen D.H. Jones's draper's shop. The photograph was taken by Mr Williams, the chemist, from the doorway of his shop.

The Rompney Castle, *c.* 1930, prior to its refurbishment during which the canopy seen in this photograph was removed.

Wentlooge Road, *c.* 1920. On the right is the Baptist chapel before the new church had been built in Ty Mawr Road. The first house on the right was home to members of the Vincent family. Rose Cottage is on the left.

The Vincent family, c. 1912. Back row: Charles (Charlie), Henry (Harry), John (Jack) and William (Bill). Middle row: Florence (Florrie), Amelia (Min) and Betty. Front row: Elizabeth, James, Hester and Lilian (Lily).

Rose Cottage, Wentlooge Road, c. 1960.

Above: Channel and Holmsview, *c.* 1913. Today these streets have been incorporated into Wentlooge Road.

Right: My younger brother Stephen North and myself in the garden of No 101 New Road in the late 1950s. The house was built by the family firm of J. North & Sons just after the Second World War and is now home to my younger son, Paul North.

This aerial photograph of the area surrounding the junction of Wentlooge Road and New Road was taken in the late 1980s. It shows the extent of the garden of Cliff North (my father) in New Road which separated his home from the builder's yard and the lane to Wentlooge Road. Both the garden and yard have long since been developed for housing but I well remember

family gatherings in the garden to celebrate bonfire nights and the memory of picking tomatoes from the greenhouse and fresh strawberries from the garden still makes my mouth water. The transport yard of T.J.E. Price is also clearly visible on the opposite side of New Road beyond the blocks of flats.

Collecting for World Peace in 1929. Back row: Thelma Rodway, Nancy Day, Mary Westcott, Pearl Giles and Mary Jenkins. Front row: Edna Turner, Gladys Williams, Joyce Trinnick, Eve John and Violet Donovan.

Two

Rumney at School

Top of Rumney Hill.

At the top of Rumney Hill, at its junction with Ty Mawr Road, stood the old schoolhouse. It was demolished for road widening c. 1966 but when this photograph was taken in 1918 there was little traffic with Rumney still very much a rural community. St Augustine's church can be seen in the background.

Once home to the headmaster Mr James Mathewson, the school house in Wentlooge Road is pictured here in 1905. The nursery school now occupies the site.

Rumney Infant School, c. 1938.

The pupils of Rumney Infant School, *c.* 1940.

Rumney schoolchildren in the 1930s.

Rumney Infant School, 1967.

Rumney schoolchildren in the 1930s. Standing are Masters Mathewson, Howells, Bolt and Williams and sitting are Masters Elliot, Fantham and Lowder.

Pupils tending the school gardens, *c.* 1940.

Rumney schoolteachers, *c.* 1935. Back row: Miss May Collier, Mr Sully, Mr Furzey, Miss Jones, -?-.
Front row: Miss Sully, Miss Morgan, Mr Jones, Miss Drazey, Miss Shapland and Miss Williams.

Rumney schoolboys, c. 1904. It is interesting to note that the boys here appear to be in uniform yet there is no apparent record of such a requirement at the time that this photograph was taken.

Rumney schoolchildren, 1925. The majority of photographs taken at this time were made by using a long-time exposure. This meant that the children had to remain still for some time – a difficult task for most! The resulting photographs often showed individuals out of focus or a deceptively sullen set of faces as in this picture.

In this Rumney school group pictured *c.* 1931 are: Dorothy Griffiths, June Proctor, Arthur Hayman, Amy Marshall, Violet Thomas, Billy John, Keith ?, Nora Williams, Mary Bowden, Joan Waters, ? Wadham, Valerie Smith, Joyce Davies, -?-, Evadne Watkiss, Delma Bradshaw, Winnie Medford, John Wells, Colin Stone, Malcolm Moss, Joy Bear, Sheila Thomas, Howard Farrell, Audrey Blower, Sylvia ?, Charlie Vincent, Mary Charles, Allen Heap, Teddy Morse, Ronnie Bristow, Len North, Audrey Richards, -?-, Joyce Penny, Mary Williams, Shirley Greenslade, Dilys Thomas, Ronnie Lucas and Sydney Norman.

Rumney schoolchildren, *c.* 1934. Cliff North can be seen in the second row from the back, third from the right, wearing braces outside his pullover!

Rumney Junior School in 1958. I am standing in the back row next but one to the form master, Mr Fieldhouse who still lives in the village. Although the faces of my classmates are very clear in my memory, to my shame all of the names are not.

Mr Jones, school master of Rumney School and a deacon of Rumney Baptist church, is seen here to the left of the group, *c.* 1920. The photographer was George Holden, a pioneer in school photography. It is not the first such photograph that I have seen where a child is holding a toy train and it is probable that the photographer used it as a prop to encourage the children to remain still.

Illtyd Vincent can be seen on the far right of the middle row in this photograph of Rumney schoolchildren from c. 1930.

Rumney School children, c. 1934. This time a little girl is holding a doll, possibly another photographer's prop.

Margaret Baldwin is sitting cross-legged to the far right of the front row in this school photograph taken at Rumney in 1942.

Rumney Junior School, Wentlooge Road, c. 1935. The school was built by Monmouthshire County Council before Rumney was incorporated into the Cardiff district.

Three

Rumney at Work

An early 1920s view of Wentlooge Road when Rumney was still very much a rural community.

Rhys Richards of Mardy farm, *c.* 1927.

In 1930, when this photograph was taken, horse-drawn deliveries were the order of the day for Harold Gosling of Sunny Bank Bakery. Harold's grandson, Brian North, continues the family baking tradition to this day.

W.R. John pictured here in Downton Rise in 1955.

The transport fleet of W.R. John & Co., October 1955. The company started trading in February 1935 in the Treorchy area selling paraffin from an improvised tanker – a large tank on the back of a lorry.

Eddie Price supervising the loading of one of his lorries, c. 1946. The lorry is a Thornycroft Trusty.

In 1946 this picture of T.J.E. Price's haulage fleet was taken on the site later to become New Road service station. Eddie Price started the business in Rumney in 1932 with one vehicle. By 1939 his fleet had grown to twelve, carrying a variety of goods. In 1949 the business was nationalised. Some years later Eddie started a new haulage business with just three vehicles and in the years that followed the business expanded to a fleet of 26 vehicles transporting goods all over the country.

Eddie Price is seen here in the centre of his workforce in 1946. From left to right: Tom Andrews, Trevor Sadler, Jack Andrews, Wilfred Sadler, Bert Young, Eddie Price, Aubrey Sadler, William Sullivan, George Jones, Wilfred Putick, Idris Price, Fred James and Dilwyn Price.

Henry George 'Harry' Vincent of Sunny Bank Dairy, with his horse Queenie, c. 1924. Before the outbreak of the Second World War Harry delivered milk as far as Roath and Plasnewydd.

William Gerrish, the Rumney butcher, is pictured here making a delivery to Mrs Phillips at the Rompney Castle before the Second World War.

Bertie Rees delivering milk for Sunny Bank Dairy in Ty Fry Avenue, *c.* 1932. A bicycle advertising Vincents can also be seen in the background.

John North (my great-grandfather). He was born in Churchstanton in Devon and moved to the Cathays area of Cardiff at the turn of the century shortly before settling in Rumney. John is pictured here in 1928 with his two sons: Alfred (my grandfather) to the left of the picture and Henry (my great-uncle) to the right.

Above: The building of Rumney Baptist church, Tyr y Sarn Road in 1929. John North and his two sons are standing to the right of the picture.

Left: Alf North, pictured here with his brother Henry celebrating the 40th anniversary of the founding, in 1913, of the family building business, J. North & Sons.

J. North & Sons works outing, *c.* 1938. These outings, often to places as far away as Blackpool, were greatly appreciated by the workforce.

Cliff North (my father) pictured in 1986 beside a Bedford tipper lorry. In the background are Melvyn Stephenson and Ken North (Cliff's brother).

"Why can't we have a nice little nest like North's build!"

She's certainly got something there—for wherever you look, in whatever direction, you'll find that North's are erecting such distinctive property. Whatever you need—from a mouse-trap to a skyscraper, give the building job to them and—relax.

J. NORTH & SONS
BUILDERS AND CONTRACTORS
144 WENTLOOG ROAD
RUMNEY · CARDIFF

This advert for J. North & Sons appeared in *Outrage*, the Cardiff University Rag magazine in 1958.

LESLIE R. BATTEN,
THE "COUNTRY" BUTCHER.
WENTLOOG ROAD, RUMNEY.

Family Purveyor for Finest Home Killed Beef, Lamb and Pork. Specialities : Red Devon Beef, Brecon Lamb Pembrokeshire Dairy-Fed Pork.
RABBITS and POULTRY (all kinds to order).

◆————————◆

CANTERBURY C.M.C. BRAND LAMB.

Orders sent to all parts of Rumney and St. Mellon's daily. Send P.C. and Roundsman will call. Join our latest Cash Bonus Scheme

The 'Country' butcher, Leslie Batten, placed this advertisement in the St Augustine's church magazine in the early 1950s.

Four

Rumney at Prayer

A Humber Hawk motor car outside the Methodist church, Wentlooge Road, c. 1960.

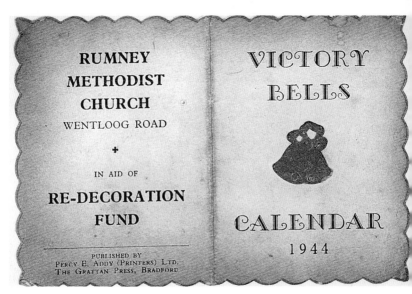

RUMNEY
METHODIST
CHURCH
WENTLOOG ROAD

✠

IN AID OF

RE-DECORATION
FUND

PUBLISHED BY
PERCY E. ADDY (PRINTERS) LTD.
THE GRATTAN PRESS, BRADFORD

VICTORY
BELLS

CALENDAR
1944

The Victory Bells calendar of 1944 was sold in aid of the Methodist church redecoration fund, one of several innovative fund-raising activities.

Gilead Wesleyan chapel, Rumney, in 1913 when Rev C. Adey Pollard was the preacher. The tithe map of 'Rompney Manor' produced in 1843 records the chapel building next to the village cross adjoining the Manor Pound and the Poor House.

One cannot fail to be impressed by the hats worn by the ladies and young girls in this group pictured outside the Wesleyan chapel at the opening of the school room in 1910.

The opening of Rumney Baptist chapel, Tyr y Sarn Road, 23 September 1929.

Rev Collier, who was minister at Rumney Baptist church from 1927 to 1937, celebrating harvest festival, *c.* 1934. I remember participating in similar festivals when my gifts of fruit were received by Rev W.J. Griffiths, who moved to Rumney in May 1939, and later by Rev D. Arthur Bowen who commenced his service in Rumney in 1955. My children were later to play their part in such festivals when Rev C. Ellis was the pastor.

The deacons of Rumney Baptist church, *c.* 1925. Standing: Messrs J. Scrivens, ? Jones, ? Bartlett, David Williams and ? Vincent. Sitting: Messrs John North, Edmund Tugwell, ? Denison and William Griffiths.

This cradle roll certificate was presented to Cliff North by Rumney Baptist Sunday school in December 1924.

The opening of the new church hall at Rumney Baptist church, 7 October 1948. The hall was officially opened by Rev Collier, who had served as minister between 1927 and 1937. From left to right: Rev Collier, Henry North, Rev Griffiths, Alf North and Mr Merry.

Dedicated to St Augustine, Rumney parish church is seen here early this century in a photograph taken from Church farm.

St Augustine's church, c. 1965, showing the lychgate which was erected by Millicent Cubitt in memory of her friend James Edward Harris who died in September 1914.

Five

Rumney in Uniform

James Vincent served in the First Battalion of the Gordon Highlanders and saw action in the Battle of Tel-el-Kebir in 1882 for which he received the Khedive Medal from Queen Victoria in person.

Above: William John Richards and his wife Penny, c. 1916.

Left: Alfred Stanley North served in France in the First World War. He is pictured here with his sister Olive in 1914.

Members of the Home Guard 'D' Company, 21st Glamorgan (Cardiff) Battalion seen here in 1943 outside the old church hall at the rear of the Carpenters Arms, Newport Road. Included in this group are Eric Evans the English master at Cardiff High School and Stewart Hallinan, solicitor.

Officers of the 21st Glamorgan (Cardiff) Battalion. Bill Hann is pictured here in the centre of the group, *c.* 1943.

The Co-operative Society shop, which was situated on Newport Road, can be seen in the background of this photograph of members of the Home Guard from *c.* 1943.

Kenneth Stanley North, c. 1939. He was a member of the Home Guard prior to serving with the RAF in India during the Second World War.

Alfred Stanley North pictured here in 1914. Alf served in France and Belgium during the First World War.

Left: Jean Sheryn North (*née* James – my mother) who served in the Women's Royal Naval Service (1945-1947).

Below: This 'welcome home' card was presented to Jean Sheryn James, by the congregation of Rumney Baptist church in 1948 to mark her safe return to the village after the war.

to you *Mrs Jean James*

Regt. *W.R.N.S.*

for your noble and self-sacrificing services through which this victory was achieved.

May God crown our glorious victory with a lasting peace !

On behalf of the Church,

W. J. GRIFFITHS,

Pastor.

The Civil Defence Corps, c. 1940. Included in the group is the then minister of Rumney Baptist church, Rev W.J. Griffiths, who is standing on the far right. Henry North can be seen at the top left of the picture.

The Great War
1914-1918.

Unveiling of Cenotaph and
Opening of Memorial Hall
at Rumney, March 19th, 1924.

Names of Fallen:

T. ABRAHAM	W. HILL
T. BAILEY	F. GILES
T. BEVAN	D. GILL
C. BRADSHAW	W. HARRIS
F. CARPENTER	H. HOWELLS
W. CHARLES	F. HOWELLS
S. COMER	C. JONES
J. CUBITT	A. C. JEFFERIES
J. DUNFORD	J. JORDAN
E. DUNN	W. LEWIS
W. GERRISH	W. MAHONEY
H. GILES	I. MATTHYSENS

J. MORGAN
J. MORGAN
G. PEACOCK
C. R. PEARSON
R. PENNY
R. RATCLIFFE
W. THOMAS
J. H. THOMPSON
H. TINKLING
E. WATTS
A. WEBBER

"Greater Love hath no man than this."

They shall not grow old as we who are
left grow old,
Age shall not weary them, nor the years
condemn.
At the going down of the sun and in the
morning,
We will remember them.   Alfred Binyon

Rumney War Memorial (Earl Haig Homes) Fund.

ROLL OF HONOUR

1939 - 1945.

R. Aberg	D. Hopes
P. Bagg	J. D. King
S. J. Baker	A. R. Lane
C. W. Barklay	G. Lane
D. Bigham	D. J. Matthews
F. L. Booth	P. Moore
W. G. Conibeare	C. A. Merrett
A. G. Connolly	L. R. Mutter
J. Crabtree	M. McLeod
F. T. Davis	I. Nelson
C. Davies	E. Palmer
L. Dowrick	S. G. H. Pain
J. H. Dunn	E. Powell
C. Emmott	A. W. Pringle
J. Evans	H. Pritchard
T. Fantham	R. Rideout
C. L. Greening	D. Thomas
G. Griffin	J. Thomas
H. E. Griffiths	P. O. Thompson
M. Griffiths	W. Toozer
F. Healy	A. Webb
M. J. Hemsley	R. Williams
R. Hicks	S. Woolf

It is a sad fact that not all who served their country in the wars returned. No fewer than 35 names are recorded on the roll of honour (1914-18) which now stands outside the Memorial Hall in Wentlooge Road. The cenotaph erected to their memory was unveiled by Lord Tredegar on 19 March 1924.

The Boys' Brigade has been represented in Rumney since 1910. The 22nd Cardiff Company is pictured here in 1955 outside the old Methodist church in Wentlooge Road. The officers sitting in the front row are Allen Hambly, Rowland Thomas and John Scurlock.

Members of the 22nd Cardiff Company of the Boys' Brigade in 1959 outside the new Methodist church. Officers at this time were Allen Hambly, Trevor Yelland, Rowland Thomas, Rev C.I. Penberthy and Cliff Barker.

My elder son James North carrying the standard
on Remembrance Day 1985 in Wentlooge Road.
Robert Nicholson is pictured to his right.

Paul North is seen here on the right helping to
carry the wreath to be laid at the War Memorial on
Wentlooge Road, Remembrance Day, 1985. Akela,
Mrs Rose, is walking to the left at the rear of
the procession.

The 1st Rumney Guides and Brownies in 1952 outside St Augustine's church. Back row: Margaret Urwin, Ann Quinn, Marilyn Morrish, Betty Radmore, Margaret Baldwin, Dorothy Lowder, Canon C.K. Smith, Mary Jones, Christine Ball and Mary Urwin. Middle row: Pat Davis, Margaret Stephens, Ann Christobel Rolfe, Carol Denzer, Gwen Hayward, Ann Sherwood, Pat Evans, Veronica Nurcombe, Merle Harvey and Ann Davies. Front row: -?-, Caroline Shepherd, Mary Lee, Maureen Cragg, Margaret Ropke, Wendy Griffin and Daphne Gregory.

Six

Rumney at Play

COUNTY CINEMA, RUMNEY, CARDIFF

The County Cinema, which was opened on Boxing Day 1939, stood at the junction of Newport Road and Wentlooge Road. I remember frequent visits to the cinema, initially as a small child for the Saturday matinée and later as a teenager when the 'County' was a popular meeting place on a Saturday evening. The cinema closed in 1974.

Left: In June 1953 the village, along with the rest of the country, celebrated the coronation of Queen Elizabeth II. This souvenir programme outlined the week's activities which included sports as well as a carnival held on Saturday 6 June.

Below: As part of the events held to celebrate the Coronation in Rumney, the children of members of the congregation at Rumney Baptist church held a party in the church hall, Tyr y Sarn Noad.

The wedding of Miss Cubitt at St Augustine's church in 1914. Harry Pacey, coachman to the bride's father, William Cubitt, is seen here in top hat. Judging by this photograph, the majority of the village would appear to have turned out to help celebrate the happy event and would certainly have helped to make it a day to remember.

The bridesmaids leaving Miss Cubitt's wedding in the car belonging to Lady Mackworth. Included in the crowd are Miss West and Miss Rawlings.

The wedding of Clifford Henry North and Jean Sheryn James (my parents) which was held at Rumney Baptist church on 6 December 1947 shortly after Cliff's discharge from the army where he had served in North Africa and Malta. In the wedding group are Alfred and Violet North, the groom's parents, with their sons, Ken, Derrick and John, and Fred and Ouida James, the bride's parents, with their son Gordon and daughter Brenda who was chief bridesmaid. The other bridesmaids were Ivy Layzell and Christine Lewis.

The North family celebrating. Standing: Alfie, Beryl (née Jenkins), Violet (née James), Cliff, Jean (née James), Ken, Eileen (née Stone), John, Thelma (née Gosling), Betty Parker (née North), Harry, Vera (née Mears), Margaret (née Jones) and Derrick. Sitting: Alf, Henry, Florrie (née Vincent) and Olive Layzell (née North).

The Rumney Show, c. 1925. Walter Morse is holding the horse for Harry Vincent of Sunny Bank Dairy.

The 'young society' of Rumney in the 1920s. The group includes Olive Jones (*née* Stephens), Edith Clease (*née* Stephens), Mr Trapnell and Gladys Trapnell (*née* Stephens). The group are obviously enjoying themselves. The men have exchanged hats with the ladies for the photograph!

Rumney football team, c. 1926. Sport has always played a significant part in the life of the residents of Rumney.

Rumney RFC in the 1958-59 season when Michael Hulbert was captain.

In 1918, despite a war still dragging on in Europe, Rumney continued to hold its traditional sports events. Many of the men of Rumney were still away fighting when this picture of a tug-of-war contest was taken on August Bank Holiday Monday. In wartime, the women of the village and surrounding areas turned their hands to many tasks previously carried out by their menfolk.

The Rumney Amateur Operatic Society, c. 1922.

This lavish production of the *Pirates of Penzance* was staged by the Rumney Operatic Society, *c.* 1936, under the direction of Walter Oaten and musical director Robert Gillard.

The Rumney Operatic Society in their production of *Tom Jones* staged in 1938. Audrey Jenkins is standing to the left of the group.

Residents of Rumney enjoying a 'D' Day celebration, 1944.

In 1945 Rumney celebrated Allied victory in the Second World War by holding street parties. This party was held in Claremont Avenue. Margaret Baldwin is at the bottom right of the picture wearing glasses. Others pictured include: Graham Rees, Joan Calvert, Mia Thomas, Elizabeth Thomas, Donald Williams, Keith Budge, Margaret Williams, Bert Baldwin, Mr Williams and Ben Rees.

A group of Rumney Townswomen's Guild members, c. 1959. In the background are Blod Morgan and Dorothy Millerchip. Sitting: Jean North, Myra Bush, Muriel Bateman, Eileen Powell, -?-, Muriel Willis, -?-.

Rumney Townswomen's Guild's 1962 Christmas dinner held at the Big Windsor in Cardiff. From left to right: Joan Collett, Myra Bush, Eileen North, Margaret North, Jean North, -?-.

Rumney Baptist church Sisterhood outing, *c.* 1958. Included in the group: 'Aunty Betty' Jones, Violet North, Florence North, Violet Nelson, Eileen Powell, Myra Bush and Audrey Jones.

Included in this Sisterhood group taken *c.* 1948 are Audrey Jenkins (*née* Sheryn), Jean North (*née* James), and Meg Sheryn (*née* Taylor).

The Rumney United Choir, c. 1940. From left to right: Sid Davies, Len Charles, Blod Prosser, Mary Noble, Eileen Powell, Evelyn Withers, Fred Morrow, Arthur Newton, ? Hill, Betty Jones, Muriel Collins, ? Rendall, Edie Davies, -?-, Margaret Dunford, Stan Truscott, Henry Rowe, Cissie Allen, Ann Bool, Mollie Edworthy, Rae Watkins, Doll Noble, Winnie Davies, Dot Vincent, ? Newton, Winnie Truscott, -?-, Martha Lewis, Kath Hulbert, Ethel Preston, ? Jones,

? Prosser, George Watkins, Sid Bevan, Bernard Noble, Trevor Withers, Allen Hambly, Tom Radford, Walter Noble, Audrey Jenkins, Dorothy Price, Ivor Jones, Bill Bateman, Ivor Moore and Lyn Amor. Tom Radford was the President of the United Choir and the conductor was Dorothy Price. Audrey Jenkins (*née* Sheryn) was the accompanist and the secretary was Ivor Jones.

Rev W.J. Griffiths is seen here with members of Rumney Baptist church Sisterhood, *c.* 1945. Others in the group include: Florence North, Mrs Marsh, Violet North, Meg Sheryn, Myra Bush, Dorothy Noble, Eileen Powell, Audrey Jenkins, Ethel Bush and Audrey Jones.

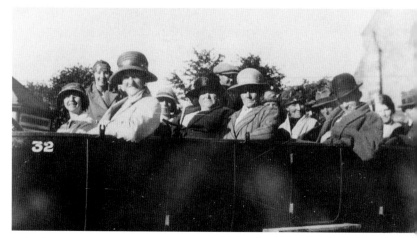

A charabanc outing, *c.* 1925. Edith Evans, Olive Stephens, Gladys Scrivens, Ivy Stephens and Mrs Hutchings are included in this group.

Seven

Leaving Rumney
and onto the Level

John North, my great-grandfather, outside the family home in Mardy Road, c. 1935. Jean North, my mother, still lives in the house although the address has now changed to New Road.

Violet North (*née* James – my grandmother) is seen here in the garden at the rear of 2 Mardy Road, *c.* 1950. With her are my great-aunt Olive Layzell (*née* North) and her daughter Elizabeth and Florence North (*née* Vincent).

The Laurels, Mardy Road, *c.* 1952.

The Level has always been susceptible to flooding and one such flood occurred on 27 May 1931. Here we see Sid Baldwin in his milk cart on the following day accompanied by Wilfred Scrivens on horseback.

Gypsy Lee of Mardy Camp is well remembered in the village to this day. Here we see members of her family c. 1970 opposite Pwll Mawr Cottages. Note the old Morris Minor car with its split windscreen, a much earlier vehicle than would appear at first glance.

Gypsy Lee at Mardy Camp, c. 1970. As a child I recall long conversations with Gypsy Lee who seemed to know everyone in the village and held me spellbound with tales of her life. She was a regular visitor to many homes in the village selling pegs and other small items.

Mardy farm in the 1920s.

Upper Newton farm in the early 1930s. Wilford Baker Jones and his family moved from Hendre Vach, St Mellons, to occupy the farm from 1929.

Middle Newton farm, *c.* 1910.

GEORGE HANDFORD. SEA BANK DAIRY FARM. RUMNEY, Nr CARDIFF

Sea Bank farm, *c.* 1912. This dairy farm was the home of George Handford.

Sluice House farm, *c.* 1967.

Sluice farm, *c.* 1967.

Above: Swy-y-mor farm, *c.* 1967. It is now derelict.

Left: The old school house which occupied the site adjacent to the Six Bells public house at Peterstone. Peterstone derives its name from the church and means the village or township of St Peter.

Horses grazing in front of the Six Bells inn, Peterstone, at the turn of the century. The Six Bells inn takes its name from the six bells housed in the tower of St Peter's church. The building was formerly almshouses belonging to the church.

The Six Bells in 1967, some sixty years later. Apart from the addition of windows and a new roof, the building appears to have changed little.

The Great Flood of 20 January 1606 is recorded by this plaque built into the wall of Peterstone church indicating the depth that the flood reached. On this occasion the water reached a height of 5ft 9in. This flood inundated the area along some 24 miles of the coast and reached four miles inland. A similar flood occurred in 1708 which covered the moors from Cardiff to Magor.

Eight

Marshfield and Castleton

A Castle class 4-6-0 locomotive passing through Marshfield station on its way to Cardiff in 1929.

The Railway Hotel, now the Port 'O' Call, seen to the rear of Marshfield station, c. 1910. The station was closed to passengers in August 1959.

Pentwyn mill, Marshfield, *c.* 1920.

Early twentieth-century Marshfield. The sender of this card, which was posted in 1907, writes 'Mary Ann's boy Willy on the road'. Who was Mary Ann and who was cousin Beth who wrote this card?

The parish church, Marshfield, 1920. The church is situated to the extreme east of the parish within a large churchyard, part of which is unconsecrated. The church is thought to have been built around 1135 and has a fine Norman doorway.

A postcard of the interior of Marshfield church, late 1920s. The church is dedicated to St Mary.

The Vicarage, Marshfield, c. 1950.

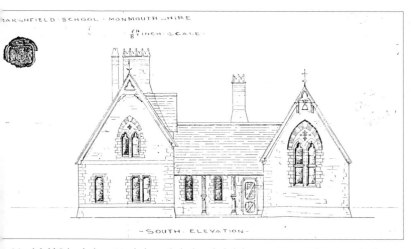

Marshfield School, the original plans of which included sleeping accommodation, was built on land owned by Sir Charles Morgan Bt. This architect's drawing was prepared by Messrs Prichard & Seddon, the diocesan architects, Llandaff.

Marshfield Road, Castleton. The Baptist church, built in 1853, can be seen to the right. Woodbine Cottage is in the centre of the picture.

Station Road, Castleton, c. 1929. Castleton, formerly known as Castell Bychan, is believed to have been the seat of the lords of Wentlooge. The castle has long since disappeared in all but name and was already in ruins in 1536 when the area was visited by John Leland.

A sale of work held in Castleton in 1920. John Jones can be seen on the far right next to Fred Jones.

A postcard of Castleton Village sent in 1912. The *Evening Post* declares 'Home Office Docks Dispute, Men Protest'.

The Coach & Horses on the right is as popular today as it was when this photograph was taken in the 1920s. The cottages in the background have long since been demolished.

Castleton village, *c.* 1920, looking westwards in the direction of Cardiff. Road widening necessitated the demolition of the cottages on the right during the 1960s.

Newport Road at its junction with Marshfield Road, *c.* 1935.

The opening of Castleton Chrysanthemum Show held in 1910.

In August 1940 the residents of Marshfield and Castleton contributed to the Spitfire Fund. Mrs Groves is pictured here in the light dress to the right of the photograph.

Nine

St Mellons

St Mellons Country Club, *c.* 1935. The house was originally Llwynarthen, the home of F.G. Evans. During the Second World War the house was owned by Sir Henry Webb Bt and was used as an auxiliary military hospital.

St Mellons village, *c.* 1928, looking towards the parish church.

Michelin tyres and the *News of the World* are among the advertisements seen in this slightly earlier photograph of St Mellons village *c.* 1920.

Ty Gollen, with its picturesque thatched roof, St Mellons, *c.* 1900.

The view of St Mellons village as seen from the doorway of the parish church in 1913.

Above: In 1914 children of St Mellons village pose for their photographs to be taken. The village was to alter dramatically with the construction of the main A48 Cardiff to Newport trunk road.

Left: The Blue Bell inn in the early 1920s. The Welsh Sunday Closing Act did not apply to Monmouthshire prior to 1921 and the public houses did a roaring trade, with the Blue Bell also offering stabling facilities!

This Christmas card advertising the Blue Bell inn was sent in 1920. The corner of the White Hart inn which was run by J. Rees can be seen to the left of the picture.

Meeting of the Tredegar Hunt at St Mellons in 1914.

Baptist Chapel, St. Mellons.

Left: St Mellons Baptist chapel, 1913.

Below: St Mellons parish church, 1914. The high ground on which the church stands provides an ideal situation from which to view the Wentlooge Level.

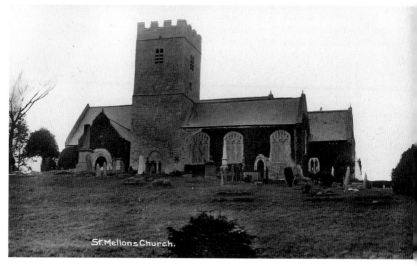

St. Mellons Church.

St. Mellons Church Lych Gate.

Right: The lychgate at St Mellons church, *c.* 1950.

Below: In September 1955 the Congregational church was rededicated. The intention was to meet the religious needs of the population of Llanrumney. Sadly, this was not to prove the case and the church was later closed.

Aston's grocer's shop, *c.* 1955. Among the advertisements are Fry's Chocolate, Bovril, Cadbury's Chocolate as well as the *Evening Standard* and *Western Mail*.

St Mellons schoolchildren, *c.* 1928. Mr Williams, the schoolmaster, can be seen top right of picture.

The opening of the YMCA hall in St Mellons in 1920.

Class 1 at St Mellons School, *c.* 1928.

A St Mellons village outing in the early 1920s.

Aerial view of St Mellons, *c.* 1965.

Ty To Maen, which was built *c.* 1880 for Mr R. Allen. The house and estate were purchased in 1925 by William Edgar Nicholls. It is a tribute to his generosity that he gave the estate to the Cardiff Royal Infirmary in 1925 for use as a convalescent home. The first patients were admitted as early as April 1926.

Patients at the William Nicholls Convalescent Home, *c.* 1946.

Staff and patients at Ty To Maen in 1930.

A Thornycroft 40-horsepower lorry leaving St Mellons village and travelling towards Rumney, *c.* 1923. At the bottom of the hill is the St Mellons war memorial.

Hill Top, St Mellons, *c.* 1908.

Quarry Hill, St Mellons. This Georgian house was built by Joseph Hemingway and was once the home of Lord Cope. The house was later used as a residential home.

Ten

Llanrumney

Llanrumney Hall, *c.* 1960. This hall was originally owned by the Morgan family of Tredegar Park before being acquired by the Williams family of Roath Court. The house and estate were purchased by Cardiff City Council in 1952. The majority of the estate was used to provide much needed housing at the time and the hall itself was established as a public house.

The building of Llanrumney Methodist church in 1959.

Members of the congregation of Llanrumney Methodist church seen during its building. The church was opened in June 1959.

The Gamekeeper's Lodge, which formed part of the Llanrumney Hall estate, *c.* 1890.

Ball Road School, Llanrumney, *c.* 1966.

Alf North, presenting a spade for the cutting of the first sod which marked the start of the building of Llanrumney Baptist church, c. 1968. The church was built by J. North & Sons.

At the bottom of Ball Road, Llanrumney, stands a footbridge over the River Rhymney. It is seen here in the snow of 1960.

Eleven

Returning to Rumney

The entrance to the Llanrumney Estate pictured from Newport Road *c.* 1960.

Witla Court, the home of the Heywood family at the turn of the century. In the 1960s the land surrounding the Court was developed for housing and the Court became a public house.

The Cross Inn, *c.* 1896. The landlord, William Lewis Rees, was also the village 'smithie'.

The Cross Inn, 1906. To the right of the picture is Wentlooge Road, at that time little more than a dirt track.

Mr Jones with a group of Rumney children thought to have been taken at Rumney Baptist church, Wentlooge Road, *c.* 1924.

This proud pigman is pictured at Mardy farm, *c.* 1925.

Rev Collier of Rumney Baptist church with members of his congregation, *c.* 1930.

Mr Mathewson of Rumney School is pictured here with members of staff and pupils in theatrical costume, *c.* 1920.

Left: A young Illtyd Vincent pictured here on horseback at the rear of No 145 Wentlooge Road, *c.* 1920.

Below: A North family outing in the early 1930s. My grandfather Alf North is pictured here behind the wheel of the family car. Standing next to him is his father John. In the rear are Alf's wife Violet (*née* James), my father Cliff, John's wife Jane (*née* Andrews) and Ken.